ADA AND THE ENGINE

BY LAUREN GUNDERSON

★

★

DRAMATISTS
PLAY SERVICE
INC.

ADA AND THE ENGINE is a Central Works Method play. It was commissioned and premiered by Central Works (Gary Graves and Jan Zvaifler, Company Co-Directors) at the Berkeley City Club on October 17, 2016. It was directed by Gary Graves, the costume design was by Tammy Berlin, the lighting design was by Gary Graves, the prop design was by Debbie Shelley, the choreography was by Travis Santell Rowland, the sound design was by Gregory Scharpen, special music was composed by the Kilbanes, and the stage manager was Vanessa Ramos. The cast was as follows:

ADA BYRON LOVELACE .... Kathryn Zdan
LADY ANABELLA BYRON/
MARY SOMMERVILLE .... Jan Zvaifler
CHARLES BABBAGE .... Kevin Clarke
LORD LOVELACE/BYRON .... Josh Schell

CHARACTERS

The play may be performed with 6 actors or 4 actors;
doubling is indicated below.

ADA BYRON LOVELACE — (18–36) Curious, funny, brilliant, aware of her brilliance, stories, aware of her story. Never met her famous father. Tries to be a "good girl" but just cannot help her curiosity and love of all things impossible. A woman of our time stuck in hers.

LADY ANABELLA BYRON — (35–55) Ada's mother, harsh strict, jealous? Yes. But realistic. She has had a hard life largely due to Ada's father. Projects his sins on her.

CHARLES BABBAGE — (40–60) Ada's soul mate, friend, mentor. Lauded genius of London. A holder of famous salons, an inventor, a mathematical scholar, a dreamer who just cannot seem to make his dreams into the metal they require to be real. Almost perfect for Ada. Almost.

LORD LOVELACE — (25–45) A gentleman who becomes Ada's husband. He'd rather that he was more rich and more lordly but he'll manage with his lot. A proud man. A wanting man. A serious man. Is not madly in love with Ada but she'll do just fine. *(Can be doubled with Byron.)*

MARY SOMMERVILLE — (40–60) Charles' friend and colleague and Ada's mentor. There are no women as successful and respected in science and math as her. Pragmatic, sharply friendly, someone who will tell you when you're wrong. *(Can be doubled with Lady Anabella Byron.)*

BYRON — (36) A charming man, darkly funny, unpredictable, emotional, brooding but self-aware. A poet.

4

SETTING

England, 1835–1852.
The Victorian era. The houses of intellectual elites.

MUSIC

Aesthetic contradiction is fun. Since the play ends with a pop rock operatic blossoming of music, the rest of the play can wrestle with an anachronistic modern sound too. The ending musical moments may be choreographically as balletic or simplistic as you like. The song is critical, however, as Ada's biggest idea was her vision of a computer writing music.

"The engine might compose elaborate and scientific pieces of music of any degree of complexity or extent."

—Ada Byron Lovelace, 1842

TRANSITIONS and LETTERS

Transitions should be active, fluid, and fun. When letters are delivered let them be in buttressed by music, choreography, or physical storytelling. Let us see the life in these letters, most of which were actually written by the historical figures themselves.

She Walks in Beauty

She walks in beauty, like the night
Of cloudless climes and starry skies;
And all that's best of dark and bright
Meet in her aspect and her eyes:
Thus mellow'd to that tender light
Which heaven to gaudy day denies.

One shade the more, one ray the less,
Had half impaired the nameless grace
Which waves in every raven tress,
Or softly lightens o'er her face;
Where thoughts serenely sweet express
How pure, how dear their dwelling-place.

And on that cheek, and o'er that brow,
So soft, so calm, yet eloquent,
The smiles that win, the tints that glow,
But tell of days in goodness spent,
A mind at peace with all below,
A heart whose love is innocent!

—Lord Byron, 1813

The Rainbow

Bow down in hope, in thanks, all ye who mourn;—
Where'in that peerless arche of radiant hues
Surpassing early tints,—the storm subdues!
Of nature's strife and tears 'tis heaven-born,
To soothe the sad, the sinning, and the forlorn;—
A lovely loving token to infuse;
The hope, the faith, that pow'r divine endures
With latent good, the woes by which we're torn.—

'Tis like a sweet repentance of the skies;
To beckon all those by sense of sin opprest,—
And prove what loveliness may spring from sighs!
A pledge:—that deep implanted in the breast
A hidden light may burn that never dies,
But bursts thro' clouds in purest hues exprest!

—Ada Byron Lovelace, 1850

"But words are things, and a small drop of ink,
Falling like dew, upon a thought, produces
That which makes thousands, perhaps millions, think."

—Lord Byron

ADA AND THE ENGINE

ACT ONE

Scene 1

Augusta Ada Byron stands in a lushly appointed room of her and her mother's house in London. She is 18, perpetually curious, slightly odd, and in an hour will be attending one of her first society events. She looks beautiful in a formal gown and jewels but doesn't look exactly comfortable in satin.

But this is Ada. And while other girls would be primping, she works on her mathematics. But how she works on maths is…musical. She hums as she works.

Then she sneaks a slim book of poems out from a hiding place.

She reads a poem that she knows by heart, but she still likes to see it on the page. Perhaps she touches it like a friend… like it's family.

The words become a simple song…

She softly taps the rhythm of the poem, its heartbeat, against her chest.

ADA. She walks in beauty like the night
Of cloudless climes and starry skies;
And all that's best of dark and bright
Meet in her aspect and her—

> *Lady Anabella Byron enters. She is Ada's mother, cold, perfect, bitter.*

ANABELLA. Ada.

Ada hides the book behind a maths text.

ADA. Yes—What?—Ready—I'm ready—Are you ready? To go? Because I am. Ready. What?

ANABELLA. You are talking. Too much. It makes the rest of us uncomfortable.

ADA. Sorry. Is it the dress? I hate this dress. Or *dresses*. As a concept they are irrationally cumbersome and weighty in their diaphanous...ness.

ANABELLA. What did I just say?

ADA. Words. Too many. Sorry.

ANABELLA. *Ada.*

ADA. Yes.

ANABELLA. What are you reading?

ADA. Nothing. Maths. The new tutor suggested I work on a geometric progression but I'd rather focus on the factorization of primes—

ANABELLA. What. Are you reading.

> *She is caught. Hands her mother the book of poems.*
> *Anabella recognizes it immediately, hates it...*
> *And starts to calmly rip out each page as she talks.*
> *Ada winces at every page.*

Daughter. We have so much against us already.

ADA. I'm so sorry, Mother.

ANABELLA. I don't think you are. I think you enjoy this rebellion. I think it lights you up, I think it fuels you.

ADA. I didn't mean to—I just found it—I didn't know it was his—

ANABELLA. This deception and defiance is at your core.

ADA. No, Mother please—

ANABELLA. Do you know *how* I come to know this?

ADA. Mother, please—

ANABELLA. Because *he* is rooted in you. You cannot help that you are his daughter—

ADA. No I cannot. Which is why I likewise cannot help my curiosity about him.

10

ANABELLA. *Know that he left you. Like any harlot he was done with.*

ADA. *Mother.*

ANABELLA. Darling if that shocks you, I'd drop the curiosity where you stand. Your father poisoned every pond he passed. He left wreckage and desperation and depravity with his every step. And I defied him. *I* did. For you. Now I know that you think you're very modern, but darling…what I had to do for you. *That* was unheard of. Women do not leave their husbands, even when their husbands are philandering, ne'er-do-well erotic obsessives.

ADA. You said he left us.

ANABELLA. He did. To wander the world from bed to bed. And yet, if I had not acted in the way I did to protect you from him fully and completely, you would have been taken from me and forced into your father's life. I fought for you in the courts, in the press. And what did he do?

He died sick and alone, mocked and sunk in the thought that no one loved him enough to save him from himself. Does that sound heroic? The genius Romantic? And yet the world gives him power through obsession.

ADA. He doesn't have any power, he's dead.

ANABELLA. That *is* power. Dead a decade and still haunts us with rumors vile and sticky. He is a constant downpour.

ADA. He's gone. Why shield me from him any longer?

ANABELLA. Not from him. From his nature in you.

ADA. I know what they say about him.

ANABELLA. Good. It's all true. The darker the truer.

ADA. They say that he was great. Flawed and—yes—dark, but a great genius of our age.

ANABELLA. Do not idealize him.

ADA. That's what we do with genius, and I hope there is some of that genius in me. I would better like to be dark and genius, than sunny and useless.

ANABELLA. You underestimate the vileness of his damage. Do not think his darkness was part of his genius. It cut his genius short, and it will do the same to you if you do not brace against it.

11

Ada hears this.

ADA. It's words, Mother. Just words. It's not an attack, it's only a poem.

ANABELLA. A poem you thought was about you, I'm sure. They all think his poems are about *them.*

That's exactly what Ada thought...

Don't be an idiot, darling. It's about some shivering bit of flesh from before you were born. I'm sure he abandoned her as soon as the lines were penned. Like you. Paste your name in a few lines, call it love, and never be seen again. That was his general *modus operandi.*

ADA. What lines? My name in his lines?

Will Anabella tell her the truth?

She finishes ripping the volume...but reserves one page.

ANABELLA. Canto Three. All for show of course. To lighten his image after he sailed away from you never to return. Who would abandon a child they loved? Who would fill a young girl's life with rumor and scandal she cannot ever escape?

Ada takes the page from Anabella and reads the passage.

Once you're married and you can't mess up your life any further, I'll answer any question you have about him, but not before. It's hard enough to find a man of worth to marry a strange girl, but more so when you have your very public lineage.

ADA. *(A fleeting edge of defiance.)* You married him, not I.

ANABELLA. *(Vicious.)* And when I see his instincts in yours I cringe, I weep, I long for the power to rip him from your fiber.

Pointed pause.

But tonight? Tonight we will give them nothing to whisper except compliments for your grace, your beauty, your deference. Tonight we prove our poise. Don't we?

ADA. Is this your debut or mine?

Anabella slaps her face.

ANABELLA. None of that cheek, my dear. That simply won't do.

ADA. Yes ma'am. I am sorry.

ANABELLA. Good. Posture.

ADA. Yes.

12

Ada straightens herself.

ANABELLA. Spin.

Ada spins for her mother to see her outfit. Small talk…

Your tutor tells me that you have almost completed the second book in the calculus series.

ADA. Yes. He is competent but not very interesting.

ANABELLA. Then let's try not to elope with this one shall we.

ADA. That was just once.

ANABELLA. For you, the difference between zero and one is your entire world.

Now. We shall have no discussion of tutors nor maths for the rest of the evening.

ADA. I'm not allowed to discuss maths at the party?

ANABELLA. Absolutely not.

ADA. But Mr. Babbage is the Lucasian Chair *of Mathematics*.

ANABELLA. I know who he is.

ADA. And Mrs. Sommerville. She has written tomes—

ANABELLA. And you are not there to discuss her tomes, you are there to find a husband.

ADA. Then why have me tutored in maths since I could talk and *not let me talk about it*.

ANABELLA. Because maths is the opposite of passion. It was necessary to direct your focus to keep you uncorrupted.

ADA. And despite your studies, he "corrupted" you.

ANABELLA. I will strike you again if you speak to me in that manner for one moment more.

ADA. And perhaps this time I will strike back.

A standoff between them.

ANABELLA. There he is. Right there. Under your skin. What must that feel like. Sickness? Itch? That's why they look at you, Ada, why they whisper. They wait to see you fall as he did. Fall into beds, into debt, into a depravity the complete description of which I have spared you thus far. And you will do well to swallow back any hint of his…steam or else you will be lost to it and die as he did, alone and unloved. That is your future if you do not present yourself the lady, find a husband with titles, and diminish. your. temper.

    Beat. Ada is…emboldened with hate for her…or just scared.

I think we're ready now.

    Anabella leaves. As we swiftly transition…
    Ada reads from that scrap of paper. Her father's words…

ADA. Is thy face like thy mother's, my fair child!
  ADA! sole daughter of my house and heart?
  When last I saw thy young blue eyes they smiled,
  And then we parted,—not as now we part,
  But with a hope.—

    Awaking with a start—

  Which lands us…

Scene 2

Babbage's House, 1 Dorset Street, London. A festive salon is bustling with London's elite. The audience are the gathered saloniste—the sound of mingling, drinking greets…

Charles Babbage, a striking man who leads with intellect and articulation. He is the gravity of the party, all drift to him. He gestures to a device offstage [unless you can build a working model]: the model of the Difference Engine.

CHARLES. Friends! Why don't we gather please. Right here, this way, thank you. Welcome and again, many thanks for your attendance tonight. For those so compelled, I offer you a glimpse at the much-discussed if-you-stand-next-to-me Difference Engine. It's only a small model of what will soon be a machine of cogs and wheels the size of a carriage. Now this machine does not dance nor chirp like some mechanical curiosities of our age, some of which you can see in the parlor. This machine calculates. But *what* it calculates and the *speed and accuracy* with which it calculates can save men thousands of hours and errors. The flawless mathematical tables it can produce by the simple turn of a crank will revolutionize navigation, industry, finance. All made better, faster, more perfect. I can bore you with the technical details, but for those ready to get back to dancing, know this... When it is manifest, and soon it will be thanks to your government's generous funding, the world will know a new way of knowing.

Now someone should hand me my rum so I stop ruining a perfectly good party.

Ada runs up through the "crowd."

ADA. Mr. Babbage. Hello. Your machine. May I ask what order of polynomial it can manage?

CHARLES. Certainly, my dear. This model can process to the third.

ADA. *(Disappointed.)* The 3rd? Oh.

CHARLES. Well. This is just a model. A fragment. The final engine can evaluate to the seventh.

ADA. A seventh order? Well that's more impressive isn't it.

CHARLES. I certainly think so. And if you care to know, the final engine would have thirty-one-digit accuracy.

ADA. *(Like "what a great song!")* Thirty-one? What a prime. I do so love primes, don't you? Lonely odd little things.

CHARLES. A description usually reserved for inventors like myself.

ADA. Oh you are no lonely inventor, Mr. Babbage. You are a titan of intellect. A genius. Are you not...*that* Mr. Babbage?

CHARLES. My pride would like to say yes but my propriety must decline that very kind praise. Did you mention your name, my dear?

ADA. No.

Which arithmetic processes does the engine employ for calculation. Does it multiply?

CHARLES. Oh no. A machine that could multiply is a far-fetched thing. The complexity would overwhelm any engine. No, the Difference Engine employs a quite useful pattern for calculating the value of a polynomial using *only addition*. The method—

ADA. The Method of Finite Differences. That's brilliant. You can use repeated addition to calculate the whole series. Well done, sir. I have heard many times of your great mind and I finally see its description was accurate.

CHARLES. That is too kind of you, miss.

ADA. It's not kind, it's true. You know some people mistake charm for brilliance. I don't.

CHARLES. That's a welcome quality in a lady. It should keep you out of trouble.

ADA. It hasn't yet. I think we should be friends.

CHARLES. Then I think we should meet. Officially. Charles Babbage.

ADA. Of course I know you. And your work. And now your house, thank you again for the party.

CHARLES. And your name, my dear?

ADA. *(Tries not to mentioned the "Byron" part.)* Oh. Well. I'm Ada… Byron.

CHARLES. Ada whom?

ADA. Byron.

    CHARLES. Byron?

        ADA. Not that Byron.

            CHARLES. *Lord* Byron?

ADA. *No.*
(Caught.) Yes.
Excuse me.

    She starts to go, stopped by his—

CHARLES. You're Mary Sommerville's friend. The young mathematician?

ADA. That I am.

CHARLES. She speaks very highly of you. She doesn't do that about many people.

ADA. Not many people deserve her praise.

CHARLES. Indeed. A pleasure to make your acquaintance, Miss Byron.

ADA. I'm am confident that my pleasure is greater. *(Switching from flattery to business a bit too quickly.)* It seems to me that the hardship

16

of producing useful mathematical tables is accounting for human error in the *transcription* of them. I find mountains of errors constantly, and I imagine it's not the *computation* that is incorrect but the *copying*.

CHARLES. The copying, yes, exactly my thought. Which led me to a simple solution for eliminating such error.

ADA. Corporal punishment.

CHARLES. No. A printer.

ADA. *(Like it's a foreign word.)* A printer?

CHARLES. Automatic and attached. All the values are recorded directly after calculation—pressed into clay—by the machine itself. No man's hands touch them which means—

ADA. Error-free calculating. Mr. Babbage. You know you might've just become, in this very moment, the single most interesting person I've ever met.

CHARLES. How old are you, Miss Byron?

ADA. Eighteen.

CHARLES. Then you've got time yet to find better.

ADA. Or perhaps I'll just have to get to know you…better.

"Is she flirting?" he thinks. "Am I flirting?" she thinks.

May I write to you? I tend to be presumptuous but you see I'm terribly good at maths and terribly bored with everything else and I sense your depth of wisdom and if you would accept my correspondence I would be most excited—Of course I understand if you are busy, which of course you are. And I am a girl of little use to you, of course I am.

CHARLES. No, my dear, no. I will admit that I do not often say this to many eighteen-year-old…socialites, but I very much look forward to our conversation. Many of them.

ADA. Yes, many. Please many.

Another pause.

Also I play piano. I'm quite good.

CHARLES. Is that right?

ADA. Yes. Music and mathematics share a language I find. Though

I also find a kind of delicious magic in music. Its ability to transport one to a most free and full place of feeling with just a few bars. I will not deny that I live for the times when I am either at my desk in study or at the keys in song. All else fades away. Freedom can look quite caged from the outside, but it's really in the mind, don't you think?

That's it. He likes her very much.

ANABELLA. *(Off.)* Ada, my dear?

ADA. Oh god.

CHARLES. Is someone calling you?

ADA. My mother. I'm off-script. Dance with me.

CHARLES. Dance with—? I don't think that's very—

Ada pulls Babbage into a waltz. With no music.
As Anabella enters...

ANABELLA. Ada, darling—

ADA. Here, Mother. Dancing. Just dancing.

Anabella sees her daughter dancing with the host. Silently.

ANABELLA. I do believe you're missing a key element of the waltz.

CHARLES. Indeed we are. You must be—

ADA. The music is in our minds, Mother. An experiment in timing.

Babbage stops dancing.

CHARLES. You must be Lady Byron. Good evening.

ANABELLA. Good evening to you, sir and I apologize for the experiment my daughter inflicts upon you, our generous host.

CHARLES. Not at all, Lady Byron. I am in your debt for the company. Your daughter is a compliment to your tutelage and taste, madame.

ANABELLA. That is very kind praise. And I am terribly sorry to leave you but— *(To Ada.)* Lord Lovelace has requested a dance, Ada.

ADA. Oh. Who?

ANABELLA. *Lord* William Lovelace, and you have accepted his request—

ADA. Have I?

ANABELLA. and Mr. Babbage has an entire house of guests to attend to.

18

CHARLES. There is truly no trouble.

ADA. The trouble is that I'm supposed to be finding a husband.

CHARLES. A worthy pursuit.

ANABELLA. And were Mr. Babbage only slightly younger I would think you were making progress at that aim.

Ada is titanically embarrassed by this.

ADA. *Mother. (To Babbage.)* That's not at all what I was— *(To Anabella.)* Mother.

CHARLES. Well. Lady Byron, age cannot be helped, can it.

ADA. I do so look forward to corresponding, Mr. Babbage.

CHARLES. As do I, Miss Byron. Enjoy the party.

Babbage exits.

ANABELLA. *Ada.*

ADA. I did not talk about maths.

Anabella turns to go—
Babbage reenters.

CHARLES. I have a book analyzing Riemann and the distribution of prime numbers that, after our discussion, I'm certain you would enjoy, Miss Byron. I'll send it over tomorrow. Good evening, ladies.

Babbage exits again.

ADA. It was only primes.

Annabella glares and whisks Ada out of the room...
And into a dance with Lord Lovelace—30 and handsome, serious, surprisingly good dancer. There is some spark between them, Ada has fun.
Babbage watches them dance from the side—aware of their youth.
Anabella watches them dance too, congratulating herself. She finds Charles...

ANABELLA. If I may sir... My daughter's is a life besmirched by gossips and a wilder side to her character that does not heed. She needs a great man like you to...speak on her behalf to young men of titles and property. She will fall to a graceless fate if she does not marry well.

CHARLES. She looks graceful to me.

ANABELLA. Yes. I think she does look happy with that one. Don't you?

> *Charles sees that she does.*
> *But Ada steals a glance at Charles. It sends a bit of a shock in him.*

> *During the dance Ada and Babbage correspond...*

CHARLES. Miss Ada Byron, I do hope you won't delay in attending another of my salons. I am sending you designs for the Difference Engine for your perusal until our conversation continues. May it be soon.

ADA. Mr. Charles Babbage, I must thank you for your letter, your invitation, and the unexpected kindness in sending the account of your Machine. I look forward to pestering you with questions and... another dance. Perhaps this time with music.

CHARLES. Miss Byron, will you join Mrs. Sommerville to dine with me next week?

ADA. Mr. Babbage, I am desperate to visit you and it might not wait till the next week. I am afraid that when an idea comes in my way I have no regard for time, space, or ordinary obstacles. Yours—

LOVELACE. Dear Miss Byron.

> *Ada and Lovelace stop dancing at this.*

I would very much like to call upon you this week at your convenience. I have thought fondly of our dance. Yours—

CHARLES. Yours—

ADA. Yours,

> *The dancing and letters lead Lovelace and Ada off as Charles hurries a note to Mary Sommerville.*

CHARLES. My Dear Mrs. Sommerville,

It was with great interest that I read your newest *Dissertation to the Mechanism of the Heavens.* I do hope we will discuss this in full at our dinner tomorrow. *(Hopefully.)* Am I to expect Miss Byron as well? *(Hopefully not...)* And her mother? Either way, I'll have much to discuss after today's meeting with the prime minister about the Engine. Yours—

> *Which slams immediately into Babbage being furious—*

Scene 3

Babbage and Mary Sommerville having cocktails at Babbage's. Mary is brilliant, takes no shit, one of Babbage's closest friends and Ada's mentor.

CHARLES. I swear to god, these crooked, idiotic ministers—these bastards—these—

SOMMERVILLE. Charles—

CHARLES. These vampires of industry, that's what they are. They are leeching the soul and the sense out of this country.

SOMMERVILLE. *Charles, really.* You're yelping like a wounded animal.

CHARLES. They took my funding, Mary. And if the government thinks they'll get this engine without it they do not realize the enemy they've made in me.

SOMMERVILLE. The government has given you more money than the Navy and all they have seen is an abacus with a crank you show off at your parties. You have to give them something.

CHARLES. I did. A model. It proves that the concept works. Now I need that funding to finish the real engine but they're saying because I haven't finished it they won't give me the funding.

ADA. It's a loop of logic.

CHARLES. It's a loop of blasted logic.

SOMMERVILLE. It's bureaucracy, Charles. You were the one that got in bed with the government. Sink into spite or fly, it's your choice.

CHARLES. Nothing is my choice. Not anymore.

SOMMERVILLE. There's always a choice. Start over, start again, do something else. All choices.

ADA. He can't abandon the engine. It will change the world.

SOMMERVILLE. If the world is ready for change. It's usually not.

CHARLES. The fact that the Engine won't be built because of some ludicrous political luddite who can't *see* the future and thus digs in his heels to prevent it from arriving, is why I much prefer automatons to people.

SOMMERVILLE. If we wanted melodrama, we would've gone to the opera. Settle yourself.

CHARLES. It must be built.

ADA. It will. It must.

CHARLES. If the government won't fund it I will do it myself.

ADA. Or with me. Take my money. Please.

SOMMERVILLE. Good lord. Your mother wouldn't hear of such a thing.

ADA. I have a dowry.

SOMMERVILLE. Which is for your husband.

ADA. But I don't have one, nor do I rather see the point. They seem at best to be boring and at worse to be cruel or tragic or...syphilitic. I shall be a bride of *science*. Babbage has lent me his designs for this Engine and I marvel at them. And not at their ingenuity, at the fact that we're waiting so long to bring it into being. I want to help that happen. Let me.

CHARLES. Thank you, my dear. I can't let you do that.

ADA. Then let me write something for the papers. I have a noticeable name, why not use it for something besides fodder for gossips.

CHARLES. I would never ask that of you, but thank you so very much. We'll find a way.

SOMMERVILLE. That we will.

ADA. I know we will. If anyone can outwit this, you can.

> *She touches his hand. Mary sees this, intervenes, taking his hand instead.*

SOMMERVILLE. We won't give up then. We might just need to give it time. But we won't give up.
Now I'm certain Ada's mother will be wondering where I've stolen her off to. We must retreat for the evening, I fear.

CHARLES. Of course you must.

SOMMERVILLE. Thank you for a fine time and the chance to scold you.

ADA. Yes thank you eversomuch. Each of our evenings together replaces the last as my favorite.

CHARLES. Thank you both for your company and patience amidst my increasingly regular fits of rage at the incompetent.

ADA. Once you've seen the future it's born. We've seen it in the Engine. And thus it will be. I'm sure of it. Good night.

> *Ada bows gorgeously, winks at him, before prancing off.*
> *Mary goes to Babbage—very serious.*

SOMMERVILLE. It won't work.

CHARLES. The Difference Engine already works in theory, and if they'd give me the money—

SOMMERVILLE. Not the engine, the *girl*. You're a brilliant man, you can't play the fool if you tried.

CHARLES. Of what exactly am I being accused?

SOMMERVILLE. She's too young for you. She's too…storied. You'll make a mockery of yourself.

CHARLES. I will do no such thing as I have no intentions in that direction whatsoever.

SOMMERVILLE. Good. She's not going to be your wife.

CHARLES. Have I ever said as much? I have *not*.

SOMMERVILLE. No you have never *said* as much. But you write her, you invite her to private dinners, you…manage her mother. That's quite beyond the pale for a friend very much her senior.

CHARLES. A friend indeed. And only that. She's an…effervescence for…the mind.

SOMMERVILLE. Oh dear.

CHARLES. Leave me be, she helps me think.

SOMMERVILLE. Your mind has needed neither help nor fizz before.

CHARLES. You introduced her to me. You mentor the child. You speak so well of her.

SOMMERVILLE. I do. As I do of you. And for both your sakes pursue her not.

CHARLES. You know me well enough to know better.

SOMMERVILLE. I do Charles. I know you. You cannot resist your next best idea.

CHARLES. I will kindly request that we only speak of mathematics for the foreseeable future, Mrs. Sommerville.

SOMMERVILLE. Alright then. *(Meaning: "Don't fall for her.")* Don't carry the one, Charles. Good night.

> *Mary leaves him. Babbage alone.*
> *He reaches for whatever wine was left and downs it.*

> *As we hear Ada's letter to Babbage…*
> *Babbage starts to sketch on his drafting table—he is on to something. A new idea. A better idea…*

ADA. Dear Mr. Babbage, I will not delay thanking you for Lardner's Trigonometry. I have had quantities of formulae to work out and have destroyed a great deal of paper in this pursuit. What can I do to help you and your marvelous machine? I do hope to see you soon. Yours truly—

> *While Ada reads Babbage's letter she prepares the room for her intended, trying to become wifely…*

CHARLES. At our last dinner you spoke of "the future." The idea of foresight has lodged itself in my temple from that evening on and I find myself in a state of intense thought. A new idea forms in me. It feels as though I stand in a valley thick with fog. I can't see where I am much less where I'm going. But the fog is lifting. A path is revealed. One step at a time I go forward into the future. I thought you would understand. Yours—

ADA. Yours,

CHARLES. Babbage.

> *Which smacks into…*

24

Scene 4

Lord Lovelace and Ada in her parlor.

This is a third or fourth date. "Date" isn't the right word. All parents and finances and reputations have conspired to bring them together for this match.

ADA. I had a thought.

LOVELACE. What kind of thought?

ADA. Well. What if you call me "bird." As a nickname. That's rather lovely isn't it?

LOVELACE. What kind of bird?

ADA. No just "bird." "Birdie." "Hello, bird!" Something.

LOVELACE. *(Trying it out.)* Hello. Bird.

ADA. And what shall I call you? Lord Eagle? Master Hawk?

LOVELACE. Hawks eat birds.

ADA. Ah yes. That would make a poor metaphor for matrimony. One hopes.

LOVELACE. Oh. My sisters wish to offer you their dressmaker for the wedding. They will make all arrangements. Silks and things.

ADA. How kind of them. Though I do have a fine dressmaker here.

LOVELACE. Theirs is better.
And I've made arrangements for a honeymoon in Ockham. Then on to Somerset. Perhaps a stop at Ashley. I thought we'd retain a London residence—

ADA. Oh we must, we absolutely must keep a home in London. Mr. Babbage's salons and Mrs. Sommerville will have us for dinners and lectures.

LOVELACE. I thought we'd be in London for the birth.

ADA. Oh. Whose?

LOVELACE. Whomever you deliver first. I rather like the name Anne for a girl, George for a boy. Children are God's gift and a man's peace of mind.

25

ADA. And lectures, I suppose, are neither.

LOVELACE. I have no opinion on lectures.

ADA. A lecture might help you find one.

A serious turn.

LOVELACE. Miss Byron. Will you be a good wife to me? I'll thank you to be honest as I know well your...lineage.

ADA. Perhaps a balanced equation is best. I will be as good to you as you are to me.

LOVELACE. It seems I must be frank. We are both aware of your need for a husband of my standing, but I need...a good wife. I am not smitten by your fame nor your father, and I will not take kindly to a life of excessive...attention. I will do everything I can to make you happy but I will expect...domesticity, integrity, fidelity. I'd like to know your mind before we proceed.

ADA. My mind? Well that you cannot have. All else, however, as is a wife's duty, I will give to a loving husband. It seems then that it is *your* mind you need to reckon with before we proceed.

LOVELACE. Yes. Well. Very good then.
And I hope you know that—that I will be devoted to you. And care for you...deeply. And—

Babbage enters, hurriedly.

CHARLES. Miss Byron. Hello. I'm so sorry to rush in.

ADA. Charles I didn't expect you until the evening.

LOVELACE. Or at all. Good day.

CHARLES. So sorry, didn't see you there. Forgive the intrusion. I took an early train. I had to. You see I think...I think I have a thought.

ADA. Oh my. Shall we walk?

LOVELACE. Now?

CHARLES. That would be most helpful. If I do not interrupt.

LOVELACE. You rather do actually—

ADA. Oh we were just chatting. You don't mind do you darling? When Charles has a thought it's best to take a turn in the garden and extract it for him.

LOVELACE. I don't see why it's so urgent—

ADA. Birds fly, that's what they do. Off we go?

CHARLES. Good day, sir. And many thanks for letting me borrow Miss Byron.

LOVELACE. Soon to be Lady Lovelace. Very soon in fact. Huzzah.

CHARLES. Oh. Isn't that…very good. I'll be in the garden.

> *Babbage exits suddenly.*

ADA. I was going to tell him. Let me tell him.

> *Ada glares at Lovelace and turns to go too—*
> *Lord Lovelace catches Ada's arm before she can leave.*

LOVELACE. I hope you don't expect Mr. Babbage to have free reign to come and go in my house?

ADA. No. But *this* house is mine.

LOVELACE. You know exactly what I mean. It's rather uncouth, don't you think, to carry on like this. I don't understand your relation to him.

ADA. Mathematical.

LOVELACE. Miss Byron.

ADA. Well I don't understand it either, but there it is. The nation's genius waiting in the garden *for me*, so I'll take my leave of you all by my little self.

LOVELACE. I fear you do not take me seriously in my objection.

ADA. To what do you object? He's my friend. Am I not allowed to keep a few of them after we marry?

LOVELACE. Not with your reputation.

> *That shuts her up.*

ADA. That's…not fair. Not at all.

LOVELACE. Forgive me.

ADA. I do not. No I don't I think I do forgive you. A gentleman would never—

LOVELACE. That was sharper than I intended.

ADA. *A gentleman would never say such a thing.*

LOVELACE. I'm sorry. My dear, I'm sorry.

ADA. No. No I'm glad you said it actually. You've wanted to throw that at me since we've met. If you think me damaged because of some stupid flirtation as a girl—or is it my father's shadow that makes you flinch. If there is darkness in me and it worries you so *then look away*. I'm not forcing you to marry me.

LOVELACE. I want to marry you. I will marry you.

ADA. He's a friend. He's just a friend.

LOVELACE. Then. We shall speak of it no more. My dear…bird.

> *Lovelace offers her a tender kiss on the cheek—*
> *Ada accepts it. And quickly turns away.*

> *A swift transition as Ada catches up to Babbage in the garden…*

CHARLES. I was in such a state about the Difference Engine. But the truth is…*that* design was never right. And I pecked at it and turned it over and over and then… A new design. A better design. So much better than the former.

ADA. But *how* is it better?

CHARLES. It would be able to perform *any* operation set for it. Not just finite differences, not just polynomials, anything.

ADA. What kind of anything?

CHARLES. Analysis. An *Analytical* Engine.

ADA. Analysis…

CHARLES. The most elaborate equations, the most complex functions, it could do them in minutes. The Difference Engine was designed to solve *one* kind of equation only. The Analytical Engine would solve anything you put to it.

ADA. But you said a machine that could *multiply* was a fantasy, much less—

CHARLES. I was wrong.

> *Pause.*

ADA. I don't think I've ever heard you say that.

CHARLES. I've never needed to.
But the Analytical Engine, as I imagine it, could multiply, divide, find roots, manage polynomials of *any* order. It could process a logarithm in the middle of dividing a hundred-digit number by a

thirty-digit number. It could multiply two fifty-digits in one minute.

ADA. Mr. Babbage, this is—

CHARLES. I know.

ADA. Charles, it's—

CHARLES. I know. The idea of a computing machine with this kind of power and flexibility? It's impossible. Until… Foresight. Pre-vision, *planning*. If you could *plan* the actions in advance, if you could *store* results until needed. Have you ever seen a Jacquard loom?

ADA. On holiday with Mother a few years ago. The most gorgeous patterns made by machine.

CHARLES. Punched cards.

> *He takes out a punch card from his pocket—a piece of card-board with holes punched in regular patterns. She takes it.*

ADA. Yes, that's how they tell the loom what patterns to weave. A hook passes through to raise a thread. No hole, no thread. Rather ingenious really.

CHARLES. For the engine. Punched cards.

ADA. Punch… Oh. *Oh.* For the operations?

CHARLES. For the operations.

ADA. For the engine?

CHARLES. For the engine.

ADA. Punched cards would let you…instruct it.

CHARLES. To do anything. Instead of weaving threads—

ADA. It would weave numbers. It would be programmable.

CHARLES. And *re*-programmable.

ADA. Change the cards, change the operation.

CHARLES. Any computation, any *combination* of computations, any time you like. It would be completely—

ADA. Universal. Charles, it would be *universal*.

CHARLES. If I can figure out how to make it work…yes it would.

ADA. Yes it would. My god. I feel like I'm witnessing the beginning of something…absolutely grand.

> *Another moment between them.*

This is a very different feeling than the one Ada has for Lovelace.

CHARLES. Do I understand that you're engaged?

ADA. Oh. Yes. I am.

CHARLES. That's cause for celebration then. Isn't it.

> *Another moment between them.*
> *Nothing can happen between them, though they both play out the consequences in their minds simultaneously.*

ADA. One question.

CHARLES. Yes, of course?

ADA. Why didn't you ask me to marry you?

> *Pause. She said it. He can't believe she said it.*

CHARLES. I don't know. I mean I *do*. I mean I…

ADA. You don't need to tell me. But there was a reason?

CHARLES. I'm sure there was one.

ADA. The difference between zero and one is the whole world. I find.

CHARLES. *(Wanting to tell her how he feels but…)* Whatever you think I am in your mind is more perfect than I could ever be. The theory of a thing is rather faultless.

ADA. The theory of a thing isn't real.

CHARLES. Some things *can* only exist in the theoretical.

ADA. Some things should be tested before they're locked up in theory. How do you know a thing won't work exactly as you'd hoped it would? Until you make it. And see.

> *They are still locked in their moment until…*

CHARLES. I should—I should—

ADA. Don't. Charles, I didn't mean—

CHARLES. I should go rest before dinner.

ADA. Please don't. You don't have to go.

CHARLES. No. But I…I should.

> *Charles backs away. It's over. As he goes to leave—*

ADA. You're going to make this new Engine. And neither of us can quantify its import when you do. And for two mathematicians that is certainly saying something. Good day.

Babbage turns—So does Ada, hiding everything spilling over inside her.
Babbage is swept away as Ada runs into...

Scene 5

Anabella. She walks in just in time to see Ada sink into a chair, deflated from disappointment.

Shockingly...instead of scolding her daughter, or straightening her posture...Anabella understands everything in a glance. She sits next to Ada, holds her. Ada bursts into tears.

ANABELLA. Darling. It's always harder for us than them. The freedom I know you want is not handed to women, even lucky ones. We must earn it, we hoard it and use it to save ourselves when the time comes. That's what I did. I used every bit of it I had to break away from your father. Now you must store it up and save it so you can save yourself if you ever need to.

ADA. That's what I'm trying to do. Love saves you. Doesn't it?

ANABELLA. *No.* Especially if you're in love with the wrong man. Please trust me that *this* is not a mistake of mine I will let you repeat.

In another corner of the house Lovelace runs into Babbage.

LOVELACE. Mr. Babbage.

CHARLES. Oh. Yes. Mr.—*Lord* Lovelace. So Sorry. Good day, sir.

LOVELACE. It was, yes.

CHARLES. Excuse me?

LOVELACE. You are a man of good standing, Mr. Babbage, highly regarded in circles I respect, so I trust that I may speak openly. My intended is a sensitive woman, prone to fits of the fantastic and the... demonstrative. Her unfortunate inheritance. Too much stimulation and I fear for her well-being.

CHARLES. You have nothing to fear from me, sir. I want only the very best of this world for her.

LOVELACE. Then leave her be.

CHARLES. Sir.

LOVELACE. Either you will. Or I will. I don't think her constitution or reputation is strong enough for the both of us. And I have neither the time nor mind to…compete. I'll thank you to excuse yourself tomorrow morning, and perhaps contain your friendship to the epistolary. For the near future. Until she gets settled in the ways of a wife. You understand. Good day.

Lovelace exits, leaving Babbage to steam a bit.

Back to Ada and Anabella.

ANABELLA. I know you think me harsh. I am. I will not let you suffer as I have. Now you must play along, marry well, and earn the freedom you so want.

ADA. Why don't the men have to earn it?

ANABELLA. Because they take what they like. For women, freedom comes with legitimacy. Marry well and then you're free. From your past, from me. Lovelace will be good to you. And we'll find him a tutor so he can carry on a conversation with you.

Ada laughs a touch at this.

He's rather good-looking.

ADA. That's true.

ANABELLA. Focus on that.

Babbage alone—perhaps he looks across the space to Ada.

And don't believe the poets. Love is either something learned or something lost. Make your choice while you have one.

Ada sits up. Breathes. Feels better.

Babbage sits down. Breathes. Feels worse.

Transition to…

Scene 6

Another series of letters pass back and forth... Ada's come as she preps for marriage.

ADA. My Dear Lord Lovelace,
I don't think there can be any earthly pleasure equal to that of reposing perfect trust and confidence in another, especially when that other is to be one's husband. I am most devotedly yours,

LOVELACE. With this you have made me the happiest of the living, my sweetest, rarest bird. In all love and, quite soon, dearest matrimony. Yours,

Babbage's letters come as he drafts, sketches, and tinkers with cogs and wheels in his study.

CHARLES. Lady Lovelace,
Though it has been months since we've spoken I thought of you when I came across the enclosed book on a recent trip to France. Congratulations on your nuptials. Sincerely,

Another as she marries Lord Lovelace...

ADA. Mr. Babbage. Alas, it has been far too long since I have written. Though I read mathematics every day, trigonometry, biquadratic equations. Though *motherhood* might diminish the time I have at my command.

Still tinkering, still in his study...

CHARLES. What a mother you will be. And no less a mathematician because of it.

She is exhausted suddenly, sitting to read...

ADA. You may have heard of the tedious illness which has occupied me since our second child arrived.

CHARLES. My dear, are you not well? Please expedite a response.

ADA. Worry not, dear friend. I am wonderfully improved, though still far from being strong.
I must confess a great happiness that you are still bearing me in mind—

CHARLES. I am grateful to hear that your health improves. I

have been invited to give a lecture in Italy this summer about the Analytical Engine at Turin.

ADA. Don't think me fairy-brained if I presume to attend the conference with you? I would be as light as air and just as quiet.

CHARLES. I've insisted that someone transcribe it. I shall see it reaches you immediately.

ADA. Thank you for the transcript. Though I'm not sure how an Englishman's lecture delivered in Italy ended up in French. I've translated it myself and am devouring it fully. Won't you come for Christmas, dear friend? Surely the machine allows you a holiday. Please come. Yours—

CHARLES. Yours—

ADA. Charles!

He looks up. Walks into a hug from Ada.
Lord Lovelace greets Babbage with a rather warm hand-shake, and Anabella bows coldly like always.

This transitions quickly into...

Scene 7

Christmas at Ada's house. Lord Lovelace and Anabella in one corner, Babbage and Ada in another.

ADA. I have never been more delighted than translating your lecture. I really did feel like myself again.

CHARLES. I'm so glad, my dear.

ADA. Not half as glad as I. You have made me so *happy* to be working again.

CHARLES. Are you not happy?

ADA. Oh no, I was. Or should be. Or *am*. I am. Children and husband and...all the things one is suppose to accomplish by a certain age. Don't listen to me babbling. How are you? I've missed you. So very much. Our time together…it always fills me up whenever I fear lacking purpose.

CHARLES. You have more purpose now than ever, Lady Lovelace.

ADA. Isn't that a funny thing. A lady.

CHARLES. And a mother.

ADA. Which is less funny. Quite overwhelming. My mind is always split. Did I ask how you're fairing?

CHARLES. You did. I'm fine. My mind is rather split as well. No matter what I put myself to I cannot stop thinking through this Engine.

ADA. Of course you can't! Nor should you! The Analytical Engine is…well it's exactly what Menabrea wrote, it's *gigantic*. A towering idea. And the separation of duties is truly brilliant. Keeping the results in the Store, while the machine processes in the Mill—it allows for a multitude of operations at once.

CHARLES. The separation is why it works at all. Any result kept in the Store may be reintegrated at any time into the Mill. And on and on.

ADA. And on and on. It's just magnificent. Your engine not only has muscle but memory. It can be taught.

CHARLES. It's the punch cards—that's the key element.

ADA. And with them, the Engine can hold the past, the present, and the future, all at once, all together in it's beating metal heart. What a thing. What an impossible thing that is suddenly so obvious.

CHARLES. You've always had your father's way with words.

Anabella heard that too. He's on her bad side, just like that.

I could have used your guidance with my lecture in Turin. Some linguistic flourish wouldn't have been missed.

ADA. Oh stop, I'm sure you were perfectly composed and obviously captivating. Menebrea wrote down everything you said. And it needs to be published.

CHARLES. It will.

ADA. It will? Oh that's wonderful. When will it?

CHARLES. If you allow them the use of *your* translation, it will be published within the year.

35

ADA. Publish…*my* translation? Mine?

CHARLES. Yes. It's rather perfect and I trust its author's expertise on that matter. The *Journal* will publish if you approve.

ADA. *Of course I do! Charles! Thank you! Oh my goodness, thank you!*

> She hugs him, Anabella disapproves from across the room, Lovelace stands and walks to them.

CHARLES. No my dear, I must thank you. Though I wonder why you didn't write an *original* paper on the subject with which you are so intimately acquainted.

ADA. An original paper? Wouldn't that be extraordinary.

LOVELACE. It appears all the excitement is in this corner.

ADA. Oh darling! Do come here. You know the lecture I was translating, the one about Babbage's engine. It's going to be published!

LOVELACE. *Your* translation?

ADA. Yes! Published! I'm going to be published!

CHARLES. Your wife's work is clear and strong and in every way an excellent specimen.

ADA. I'm an excellent specimen! Isn't that lovely! Could there be a prouder husband?

LOVELACE. There most certainly could not.

ADA. Then he approves of his wife, the authoress?

LOVELACE. Of course I do. I certainly do.

CHARLES. Your heritage would indicate such a fate most likely.

ADA. But mine shall be the poetry of science. Less rhyming, more calculus.

CHARLES. Speaking of which. I was wondering if, along with the translation, you might perhaps add some further explanation of the machine, some notes to give greater context and—

ADA. Oh yes I must. There is a noticeable lack of philosophic explanation that I could readily remedy. Perhaps a table, a diagram of some sort, some way to show exactly how the engine would think, step by step.

LOVELACE. Does it *think*? Can it *think*?

ADA. Of course.
I mean not exactly *think*, but *process* thought—
Exactly.

CHARLES. Not exactly.
Well yes it *thinks*, in that it processes—
Precisely.

LOVELACE. Precisely...what?

ADA. I'm so sorry darling, we're boring *and* confusing and you can only be one of those in polite society.

CHARLES. Apologies, Lord Lovelace.

LOVELACE. No no. It's a certain kind of pleasure to see my bird so... animated again.

ADA. Nothing animates like mathematics. I cannot wait to get started on this. Thank you. *Both.*

CHARLES.
Of course, my dear.

LOVELACE.
Of course.

>   *Odd, brief pause.*

LOVELACE. *(Changing the subject.)* What does it look like?

ADA. What does what look like?

LOVELACE. The—what is it—Algebraical—

ADA. *Analytical.*

LOVELACE. *Analytical* Engine? Yes. What does it actually...*look* like?

CHARLES. Well. It's not built as of yet, but when it is.

ADA. And it will.

CHARLES. It will be a rather large—a *very* large, steel and brass and steam-powered...um...

ADA. *Loom.*

LOVELACE. A loom?

CHARLES. Yes.

ADA. But the size of a ballroom.

LOVELACE. A loom as big as a ballroom?

CHARLES. Bigger. It could go on forever really, the more gears one adds, the more work it can do.

ADA. And I suppose there's nothing stopping you from adding more—

CHARLES. And more—

37

ADA. And more processing power. Columns of steel and steam—

LOVELACE. What's in the columns then?

CHARLES. The numbers. On gears.

ADA. Falling into line as the engine thinks and thinks.

LOVELACE. So it's a *thinking* loom?

ADA. With the heart of a train. Loud like a train too. Clanging and smacking, always beating and pushing, metal into metal.

CHARLES. Gears locking into gears.

ADA. Cogs in columns, then dropping

She claps.

from one column into another—

She claps.

CHARLES. The noise.

ADA. The noise would be titanic, wouldn't it?

CHARLES. But rhythmic.

ADA. Yes.

CHARLES. For if it has the heart of a train it has the nerves of a clock.

ADA. Ticking and clicking, but not so regular as time passing.

CHARLES. No. As the information passes through the machine towards its solution, entire sections of the Mill—

ADA. That's where the "thinking" is done.

CHARLES. Yes, those sections would shudder and convulse—

LOVELACE. Convulse?

ADA. With waves of switches flipping and spinning down its back like tumbling water but not water, *information*, decimals, symbols flowing and gliding and dancing—

LOVELACE. Now it's dancing?

CHARLES. Information switching partners—

ADA. changing hands—

CHARLES. converging and iterating—

ADA. Pirouetting and processing until—

CHARLES. It stops.

38

ADA. It stops.

Pause.

LOVELACE. What happens when it stops?

CHARLES. Well it's either finished its job or it's broken.

Babbage and Ada laugh, Lovelace tries to. Realizes he's out of his element.

Anabella walks over.

ANABELLA. Ada darling, I believe it's time to bid your children good night.

ADA. My goodness the day has flown by. Excuse me, gentlemen. When I return I shall force Mr. Babbage to describe the Engine's operations transfer in full.

LOVELACE. Over dinner?

ADA. It's for the paper.

Ada steps away giddy—until her mother pulls Ada aside—

ANABELLA. It's getting a bit explicit, darling. The giddiness. Your husband is in the room and you're fawning over another man.

ADA. I'm not fawning, Mother, please.

ANABELLA. Babbage's letters have been constant, as *I'm sure* has been his affection. I only caution you—

ADA. *Mother, we're working together. I'll have no more of this in his presence nor in my house.*

ANABELLA. You'd think he would have left you alone now that you're married.

ADA. Wasn't that supposed to be our arrangement?

Ada walks away from her mother, who exits too.

Lord Lovelace and Babbage chat.

LOVELACE. Your letters gave her great joy. And now this. I haven't seen her this lifted in ages. I thank you for it.

CHARLES. You are most welcome. I hope you don't mind the correspondence.

LOVELACE. I did not and do not. And I...I really must apologize to you, sir. For our last encounter. You have been a great friend to

39

her and a steadfast supporter and I hope you can forgive my...over-emphatic slight. She is lucky to have you as a friend. As am I.

CHARLES. Well. That's very kind.

LOVELACE. You see the births were not altogether easy on her, her health has always been poor, but your correspondence strengthened her throughout her trials.

CHARLES. And I am grateful for that strength as it is I who take strength from her. She has a kind of...electricity to her.

LOVELACE. *She* certainly thinks so.

CHARLES. It is hard to deny. She truly is...

LOVELACE. Yes she is. Though I always feel I need your aptitude for mathematics to fully deserve her.

CHARLES. Oh no... No.

    Pause. Though they both know it's true.

LOVELACE. Love is a changeable thing is it not?
The more life we share, the more I care for her. We were in...agreement before. But now I do think we are in love...of a kind. My understanding was that it went the other way around, but I suppose I don't care which way it goes as long as she is happy.

CHARLES. She seems happy to me.

LOVELACE. Does she? Good. I hope it strengthens evermore until, as they say, death do us part.

CHARLES. I will tell you, love does not stop at death. Once you share a life, especially children, the soul...*compounds* itself. My wife is always near to me even now.

LOVELACE. Excuse my ignorance. I did not know you were once married.

CHARLES. Yes. Georgiana. She was so young when she died, she wouldn't recognize me now. That's an odd thought isn't it?

LOVELACE. Good women. Make for better men. Something like that.

    These men are both talking about Ada and know it. Pause.

Would you tell me what a logarithm is?

    Pause.

CHARLES. You might ask your wife.

Ada enters—

ADA. The boys are destroying your very kind gift, Charles, but then again that seems to be what boys do with everything—

LOVELACE. Darling?

ADA. Yes, dear?

> *Lovelace has walked right up to his wife and kisses her, sweeps her into his arms and kisses her.*
> *Ada did not see that coming. Neither did Babbage. Neither did Lovelace really.*
> *When he lets her up, she takes a breath.*
> *Babbage doesn't know what to say—so he raises his glass to them both as…*
> *The next scene sweeps in.*

Scene 8

Letters pouring out of Ada to Babbage.

ADA. My Dear Babbage, I am working very hard for you, like the Devil in fact, which perhaps I am. I have made some very important extensions and improvements to the processing.

> *Another letter—Lord Lovelace joins her, helping.*

You will admire the table and diagram extremely. Lord L is at this moment kindly inking it over for me. He is quite enchanted with the beauty and symmetry of it.

LOVELACE. Birdie. Is this to your liking or—

ADA. NoNoNo. He's got to be able to read it, darling. Please summon up your best handwriting.

LOVELACE. This is my best.

ADA. Then summon up someone else's.

> *Another letter as Lovelace exits with his papers.*

It must be a very pleasant thing to have Fairy in one's service—I, poor Fairy, can only get mortals to wait on me.

41

Another letter.

I have made Lord L laugh by referring to this paper as my child. I think he is an uncommonly fine baby.

Another letter.

You know I do not believe that my father was such a poet as I shall be an Analyst.

Another letter.

Enclosed is our revised and corrected translation and notes in its entirety.

Your Fairy forever,
Ada

> *And suddenly they are met.*
> *In Babbage's office. Evening.*
> *Babbage reviews her work.*

CHARLES. *Sketch of the Analytical Engine Invented by Charles Babbage.*

ADA. *With Notes by the Translator...*

> *Charles holds up a thick stack of papers.*

CHARLES. Good lord. Your notes are twice the length of the translation.

ADA. *Thrice.*

> *Babbage reads.*
> *Ada waits for him. She fidgets, anxious.*
> *Points out and reads aloud to make sure he's seeing it.*

This bit's rather good I think: "The Engine is not merely adapted for *tabulating* the results of one particular function, but for *developing and tabulating* any function whatever."

CHARLES. Uh-hmm.

ADA. "A new, a vast, and a powerful language is developed for the future use of analysis—"

CHARLES. Yes I can—

ADA. "With commands input via punch cards, there is no limit either to the magnitude or the quantity of numbers used—"

CHARLES. I am reading it.

ADA. And the diagrams I think turned out quite well. Producing the

Bernoulli numbers proves that the engine can do anything mathematical. Most professors cannot manage Bernoulli but *it* can—I proved it can.

The program I laid out— *(Pointing out the diagram.)* is flawless. Because I found one of your flaws by the way. Carry the one, Charles.

Now I set down every command given through the punch cards and every corresponding step the engines would take in a calculation of this complexity.

Silence. Babbage engrossed, Ada anxious.

And I know you don't particularly agree but, as a small gift to myself, I might have snuck in the bit about the Engine one day writing songs.

CHARLES. "Supposing that the fundamental relations of pitched sounds were input, the engine might compose elaborate and scientific pieces of music."

ADA. Yes. I rather love that thought. A singing machine.

Pause as Babbage says nothing. Lost in the pages.

I might combust if you don't say something. I've worked so hard, and I think it's quite brilliant, and as far as I know this work is unheard of—

He looks up.

CHARLES. It's perfect. Pray do not alter it. Not one word. All this was impossible for you to know by intuition. Yet you know it as thoroughly as I. Greater than I. You see its…future.

ADA. I do.

CHARLES. And the music.

ADA. Well. If the engine can process numerical commands it could theoretically process any symbol. Notes instead of numbers is what I see.

CHARLES. Yes. Notes, numbers, it makes perfect sense.

ADA. Does it?

CHARLES. Over and over again, you surprise me. You shock.

ADA. Don't I sound…alarming.

She is so relieved and happy that he liked her work.
He is so impressed and amazed.
If he were a different kind of man, he would have swept her

43

off her feet and kissed her.

She would rather that he was that kind of man. They are both imagining that which they cannot seem to make themselves do, but want to do very very much.

Babbage comes closer to her, Ada babbles instead of addressing him.

There are only a few more corrections for the printers. They rather insist on capitalizing all my subscripts which quite alters the meaning of B_{2n-1}. *(Read as: "B sub 2, n minus 1.")*

He is calm even with the electricity coursing between them.

CHARLES. I hope you know...how grateful I am for you. And how much I...

I hope you know.

ADA. I do. As must you. Know.

They should be making out right now...but they aren't. They can't.

Actually they could...but they won't. Stuck in the middle of want and won't.

Ada tries to break the gravity of the moment.

Then...we should both be...quite satisfied with ourselves. Our work. The paper. Which truly is the best of both of us. We have finally made manifest so many conversations. Our collective dream it seems is... real. We are, in this respect...complete.

CHARLES. Complete.

ADA. Yes.

CHARLES. Partners really.

ADA. Partners?

CHARLES. In this respect.

ADA. Oh. Yes.

CHARLES. Yes.

Their breath is the only thing moving in the room. Breath. Breath.

ADA. I'm so sorry.

44

Ada turns to go—but Charles reaches out and catches her hand quickly and surely. He's not letting her go this time.

She spins back to face him. Then steps forward towards him. Perhaps he touches her cheek or arm. If he does she lets herself enjoy this for an instant before going back to thinking, "I should leave right now even though I don't want to."

This is the closest they can get to each other in this world. The most intimacy they can manage. All tension and electricity between them has this one single, silent channel. Eyes on eyes, hand on hand, breath so very close to breath. Perhaps he opens his mouth to speak the impossible when—

Blackout.

End of Act One

ACT TWO

Scene 1

Exactly where we left them.

The energy, the want, the impossibility flowing between them like Faraday's electricity.

Hand in hand.

ADA. *(A small voice.)* I do…I have…I have to go.

CHARLES. You *have* to?

ADA. I have to go.

CHARLES. Ada. Just—

ADA. I must. A train. Catching a train.

CHARLES. Ada—

ADA. I can't—

CHARLES. Please.

ADA. I'm sorry. I'm so sorry. I can't. I must go. I really must.

She releases her hand. Apologizing without words.

He nods—perhaps clears his throat. Busies himself in the room somehow. Trying to accept that they won't be talking about their relationship or… Babbage moves back to business, partly to change the subject, partly to recover from some embarrassment.

CHARLES. Of course. And I won't keep you longer than to broach one more issue before you go, if I may.

ADA. Charles.

CHARLES. NoNo. I just have a small preface that I wish to see attached to the paper. A short note really. A small introduction to

46

the piece, then your translation, then your marvelous notes.

ADA. What sort of preface?

CHARLES. Just—context. Contextualize the engine, its development, its varied history.

ADA. Has it had a varied history?

CHARLES. You'll understand when you see it. I do have the draft here somewhere. Where is the damned thing? I'll find it. Here it is. Good.

He gives it to her to read.

It will, I think, add a touch of weight to your paper and some frankly *necessary* blame for the great delay in seeing this work come to its proper fruition.

ADA. Forgive me, you mean to preface the paper with *this* letter? To be published in the journal as well.

CHARLES. Well yes. The scientific community will, I think, be interested in the sightless ministers of this crooked government who defunded the Difference Engine to the great loss of this country.

ADA. Charles.

CHARLES. The Difference Engine would have been made if not for the prime minister's complete lack of—

ADA. *Don't do this. This is lunacy.*

CHARLES. Lunacy. I beg your pardon.

ADA. *(Reading from his note.)* "The viability of the Difference Engine was without question, even as its first breath was squeezed out by this government's miserly—" Charles, really. You cannot be serious in this. To print this is to shame the government with common libel.

CHARLES. It is not libel, you know it's not, it's a short statement of only true facts and justifiable opinion.

ADA. Is it signed?

CHARLES. What.

ADA. Is this short statement signed. by you?

CHARLES. Well the paper is yours, yours and Menebrea's, not mine.

ADA. So you would have me put *my name* behind this?

CHARLES. I am not asking you to claim it as yours.

47

ADA. By not claiming it as *yours*, yes you are. This good work, *my* good work, that took months of my time and you would tarnish it with such foolish name-calling that everyone will know comes from you no matter whose name you put behind it.

CHARLES. *They didn't fund it because they're sightless and cheap and they need to be pilloried and mocked for it, not reelected.* These ministers are doing damage to the intellectual vibrancy of this nation and they cannot survive if they mock me, they will never mock me again.

ADA. Then stop making it easy for them.

CHARLES. If this information seems to come from me they won't listen.

ADA. And if it seems to come from me it's a lie.

CHARLES. You can't refuse me on this.

ADA. Excuse me.

CHARLES. You cannot.

ADA. Oh I very well can *and will.*

CHARLES. You will print it, yes you will, it will be printed as I laid it out.

ADA. I will never let it hit the page.

CHARLES. This I did not expect. That you would end up like the rest of them, burning the bridge as I cross it.

ADA. I'm saving you heaps of embarrassment. The publishers will never consent to printing it either.

CHARLES. Then you will retract the paper from such idiot purveyors.

ADA. I will *retract this paper? From print?* Who are you? Who would have me efface months' worth of work and time and, if I do say, *leaps of mental acuity* in translating not just the French but your knotted complexity into the vernacular of reality. You would tell your friend to simply retract it?

CHARLES. If she were a real friend, she'd do it without question.

     Pause. Ada is steaming.

ADA. I am. Your very best friend. And thus I cannot and will not support you in acting in a manner not only wrong but suicidal.

CHARLES. You defy me then?

ADA. Is it not *you* who defy *me*? *My good sense?*

CHARLES. Oh yes, *sense* is your family's most rumored feature.

ADA. Do not condescend to me when you are using my name to sell your lies and you know it. I am a prize for you. I am your protégé. And I am every bit the genius you are.

CHARLES. So you keep telling everyone.

She almost laughs at this. Then she's serious and leaves.

ADA. I see we have turned a corner that I fear will lead us off a cliff. I will see myself out, Mr. Babbage.

CHARLES. Yes you wouldn't want to "miss your train."

Like a flicked switched she changes her mind to stay and fight.

ADA. Do not punish me for protecting us.

CHARLES. From what?

ADA. *Each other.*

CHARLES. I don't need your protection, my dear. Not from myself and not from a socialite.

ADA. Oh my *mind* you'll employ when it serves you, unless the woman attached to it *objects* to a ludicrous thing, then? Then you dismiss her as turncoat fool. Well if you think I would be so easy manipulated you know me not.

CHARLES. And yet you've done everything I've asked so far.

ADA. Then it's a good thing you're too scared to ask for the thing you actually want.

She means herself of course. Slam.

CHARLES. It's my engine, Ada.

ADA. It's my program, Charles. My work.

CHARLES. *Your work is my work, this work, this idea, everything in this is mine first. It doesn't exist without me and neither do you.*

Oh damn.

ADA. Like your engines? Do they *exist*? I have yet to see them. The designs of which you boast exuberantly would beg the question… where are the machines themselves? Why does not the great man, with the great ideas, produce any *great thing*? Why? Because you're scared.

CHARLES. Of you?

ADA. Of yourself, you coward.

CHARLES. *Coward?*

ADA. Perhaps you hate these ministers because you fear they're right. You can't be trusted to produce anything but promises. Oh. *And models.*

CHARLES. I could say so much worse of you.

ADA. OH yes, the girl with sin in her blood, who talks and dreams and leans in so much closer than other girls do. Is a Romantic worse than a coward?

CHARLES. I am not a coward.

ADA. *You are scared of your best ideas!* This engine could be made. It should be made. And if it's not made? It will be because of your cowardice and the fact that you turn on your friends.

CHARLES. My friends turn on me, they always do.

ADA. You're an ass, Charles. *You* are the thing in your own way. You stop yourself. A mountain of your best ideas weigh nothing if they are not made, and because of some counterproductive form of perfectionism *they die in your mind.*

CHARLES. I won't bring something into being if it's not perfect. If it's not perfect why do it?

ADA. That's a clean way for a coward to sound like a hero.

CHARLES. *I am not a coward.*

ADA. You're scared of everything except what's in your head. And that is where your best ideas are buried, unmade and unmet.

CHARLES. You've lost your mind and your decorum and you're not making any sense.

ADA. *(Talking about them.)* And You. Make. Nothing. You dream, you promise, and nothing comes of it, and it's all for naught, and you could remake the world but you're terrified of seeing your dreams in the daylight.

> *Ada goes to leave finally but falters—a wave of pain in her stomach comes over her so strongly that she freezes to weather it.*

CHARLES. What. Ada?

With a firm hand she stops him.

ADA. *(Holding her rage down to a low flame, but it is a hot one.) Do not. Touch me.*

Here is the truth of things. We need each other.

CHARLES. My dear—

ADA. I am speaking. You are brilliant but unpleasant. I am brilliant but unrecognized. I see only one solution to both save you from yourself, and me from mediocrity: We must continue to work together. Partners is what you said, and I agree.

CHARLES. I did not mean ours as a business arrangement.

ADA. What if it was?

    Pause.

All I want is for the engine to be built, that's what I've always wanted. If I could craft it such that you would do nothing but engineer it into existence, would you let me manage everything else? Let me do that work, while you yours. Partners.

CHARLES. You call me a coward and then you propose to work for me?

ADA. Well you would really work for me.

CHARLES. *Are you mad.*

ADA. That's not what I meant. I meant that I could manage the money, the relationships, the business—and if any of your machines are to be made there must be a *business to it.*

CHARLES. And you would *manage* me? Keep me in check, make sure I played nice.

ADA. *Exactly.*

CHARLES. *Exactly not. No. Never.*

ADA. A bit of *management* could take you from zero to one. The entire universe is in their difference.

CHARLES. *If you think small enough.* This is impossible.

ADA. A thinking machine was impossible until *we* told them how it could be done.

CHARLES. It doesn't think, it takes orders. *(Talking about her.)* Therein lies its value.

51

My dear you are out of your depth here. Not least by speaking to me like I am an overactive child you need to keep busy lest they ruin the wallpaper. Secondly, I would never, in a millennia, trust you to manage my money when I have consoled you on your gambling losses more than once.

ADA. *The algorithm was correct, the HORSES were wrong.*
And I was trying to raise money for you.

CHARLES. Well stop it. You're embarrassing yourself and me by association. What I need instead of your questionable financial and entrepreneurial guidance is time. Time is what I want. I need peace of mind to talk to the damn thing, and time to listen.

ADA. We don't have time.

CHARLES. *We* don't have anything, you and I. *We* don't.

ADA. No we don't. Neither friendship, nor sense, nor time, nor the years that we want *to realize this dream, we don't have it, we have nothing, nothing, nothing left and no time TO MAKE ANYTHING REAL.*

> *Her outburst drains her into breathlessness. Ada leans on something. Charles is now concerned for her. What's she really talking about?*
>
> *Then in a flash Ada cramps so hard that it stops her in full, bends her over—she manages it quietly, but he sees her pain. He steps to her, she waves him off again. It passes.*

CHARLES. My dear you must tell right now what's wrong.

ADA. Oh. A bit of everything at the moment.

CHARLES. Ada. What is this?

ADA. Something like…the beginning of the end. The doctors—I think they're placing bets on whether I survive the winter.

CHARLES. The winter? What on earth are talking about?

ADA. It's what I've been battling for years. And it seems it's winning. I'm told there's little for it but prayer and laudanum.

CHARLES. No.

ADA. Neither of which make me think straight.

CHARLES. No that's not right.

ADA. You know my father died at 36.

CHARLES. Ada, no.

ADA. I'll be 35 next month.

> *Babbage drops every rule of his time and grabs her into a hug— an embrace that is shock and desperation and dependence and love and sadness.*
>
> *She holds him back. Releases into him. Grips him, embraces him, needs him.*
>
> *We see how scared she really is.*
>
> *After a moment he whispers something to her—we can't hear it—but she nods, thanks him with this. Perhaps he told her that he loves her. She is so imbued by whatever he said that she is speechless, exhausted, vulnerable.*
>
> *They sit together. Closer than they ever have been.*

I'm still mad at you.

CHARLES. Good. I'm still mad at you.

ADA. Good. Because I won't accept your pity.

CHARLES. Well, pity's for strangers. What I have for you is a plan. I have doctors, I have friends at the medical school. And I have a commandable, programmable calculating machine that might or might not write an opera. And it must be built.

> *She likes the sound of that…even though she thinks she won't see it built.*
> *Babbage sees this too.*

We also must plan to visit the Great Exhibition next month. A world's fair of technology and industry. Inventors for miles. You'll love it.

ADA. I've heard they're covering Hyde Park in glass.

CHARLES. Yes, the Crystal Palace. A fine design. I could've done it better. Still. Steel and glass and a hundred thousand people inside. And we will go. And see the future together.

> *She really does love that idea.*

ADA. Please don't leave. I fear it will get bad. Byrons don't seem to die easily.

CHARLES. You are not your father.

ADA. I think of him so much now. It feels like memory, but I never knew him. And yet I…I do know him…somehow. I know that he died alone. Which is my greatest and growing fear.

CHARLES. You are not alone.

ADA. When it gets bad and I am not myself, please don't leave me, please.

CHARLES. I won't, my dear.

ADA. Please, Charles.

CHARLES. How could I leave. You're far too interesting. And you're the only one who understands me.

ADA. *And* puts up with you.
Did you know that you said you wanted time to "talk to the Engine"? Did you know you said that?

CHARLES. Said what?

ADA. You said "I want time to talk to the damn thing." You meant the Engine.

CHARLES. No, I didn't, I didn't say that.

ADA. Yes you did, I heard it clear as day. You're a bit poetic after all, talking to inanimate objects.

CHARLES. *(Teasing now.)* Hush you.

ADA. Hush *you*, titanically rude malcontent.

CHARLES. I'm a malcontent if you're a—

ADA. What am I? Tell me.

CHARLES. A…harpy, of some sort, I don't know.

She laughs just a little at him. He laughs at himself.

ADA. I'm a bird.

CHARLES. Not a fairy?

ADA. I suppose both have wings. I made wings once as a girl. Almost dove off the roof if the nanny hadn't grabbed me. Though I like to think I would've flown. Or perhaps I am just a flightless bird.

54

CHARLES. An emu.

ADA. Did you say emu?

CHARLES. Flightless bird. You said.

ADA. You're calling me an emu?

CHARLES. I'm not, you're calling you an emu.

ADA. That's the worst thing anyone has ever said to me.

CHARLES. I didn't say it, you did.

ADA. No gentleman should call a lady an emu.

> *Does Charles do an "emu" gesture, whatever that is? If he*
> *does, she laughs at it.*
> *A moment.*

CHARLES. What can I give you, Lady Lovelace?

> *Pause.*

ADA. All the impossible things. And hurry.

> *He looks at her...she looks into the great grand future in her*
> *mind.*

Scene 2

> *A letter from Babbage takes over—though perhaps they do not*
> *move an inch from the previous moment. They sit together, he*
> *holds her, they both look out...*

CHARLES. My Dear Ada,

> *Lovelace appears, unsettled, upset. He is in the near future*
> *while Babbage and Ada are holding fast to the present.*

LOVELACE. Dearest Lady Byron,

CHARLES. I find it quite in vain to wait until I have leisure so I have resolved that I will leave all other things undone and set out for you—

LOVELACE. Your daughter's health slips in rapid decline. Her pain brings her fits of either howling or whimpers. The laudanum is the only tool I have to calm her.

CHARLES. I take with me papers enough to enable me to forget this world and all its troubles and if possible its multitudinous charlatans—everything in short but the Enchantress of Numbers.

LOVELACE. She is not as she once was. I know not how to help her.

A letter from Ada.

ADA. Dear Babbage, I write to entreat that you will act as my executor in the event of my sudden decease. No mutual knowledge of any two human beings in this life can give such stable ground for faith and confidence as ours.

LOVELACE. As her mother I ask you to consider joining us in residence to ease her end.

ADA. Most affectionately,

CHARLES. Farewell my dear and much admired Interpretess.

LOVELACE. With haste,

CHARLES. Evermost truly yours—

And now Anabella directs a letter at Babbage.

ANABELLA. Mr. Babbage.

Ada is grabbed by her mother from Charles.

My daughter is not well and not improving. I am left to manage her affairs as she is no longer capable.

Lovelace helps Ada across the room and administers her laudanum.

From a brown bottle he drops many drops of the liquid into a glass of water. She drinks it, breathing through her pain. After she downs the drink she relaxes—sleepy—high.

I ask you to leave her in peace. Let me be clear. You are not welcome here any longer.

The letter ceases as Babbage confronts Anabella at the door to Ada's room.

CHARLES. Lady Byron, you've known me almost twenty years now, you know my deep concern for your family, you cannot push me out.

ANABELLA. Your concern has always been, even when deeply inappropriate, for my daughter, who is no longer accepting visitors.

CHARLES. I am not a visitor. I'm the executor of her will.

ANABELLA. I don't care what honorifics she threw at you while in one of her stupors. You are not family and not welcome.

CHARLES. I insist on seeing her.

ANABELLA. You may insist, Mr. Babbage, but you will not enter.

CHARLES. I know you are writing letters in her name. I know her hand and this is not it.

ANABELLA. She cannot do it herself.

CHARLES. *And she would not want you speaking for her.*

> *Lovelace joins Lady Byron.*

ANABELLA. Mr. Babbage.

LOVELACE. Mr. Babbage. Your concern is noted. Thank you. And please leave.

CHARLES. Sir. I was explaining to Lady Byron that I—

LOVELACE. *(Explosively.) Please leave, sir. She is no longer your concern, nor your puppet, nor the woman you, nor any of us, knew her to be. There is nothing for you here. Good day.*

> *Babbage doesn't know what to do but leave...*

> *A breath.*
> *Ada and her mother and husband. Ada is high and delirious on the couch.*

ANABELLA. Coming around almost every day now. No propriety at all.

LOVELACE. I don't really care about propriety at the moment. I just want peace. I want her well.

ANABELLA. She's not going to be well. Not ever again. We must hold fast to etiquette.

LOVELACE. Etiquette does not help her pain. She's drowning in it.

ANABELLA. Well. She doesn't talk to the deacon, she doesn't pray, she refused the mesmerist I sent, she doesn't even get off the couch—

LOVELACE. She *can't stand.*

ANABELLA. You push that drink down her throat all day—

LOVELACE. It's the only way she sleeps, it's the only thing that helps her pain.

ANABELLA. *Suffering is the price we pay for sin.*
It is not elegant, but it is sometimes necessary. Only God can forgive and relieve us.

ADA. *(Oblivious.)* Excuse me.

LOVELACE. Good thing He gave us opiates.

ADA. *(Going for more laudanum.)* Excuse me.

LOVELACE. And no more of your deacon round this house, I'm sick of it. Evangelists and mesmerists do not help her.

ANABELLA. Then she cannot be helped.

ADA. Excuse me.

LOVELACE. *(To Ada.)* Yes. I'm sorry. Yes, dear.

ADA. We shall be late for the Exhibition if we do not collect ourselves at once. All of our friends will be there. At the Crystal Palace.

LOVELACE. She's been talking of the Great Exhibition all week. She thinks it's last year.

ADA. Charles will meet us at the grand fountain.

LOVELACE. Ada. The Exhibition is over.

ANABELLA. And there shall be no more mention of Mr. Babbage.

ADA. But we're going to see the displays of industry and technology. The Crystal Palace is all light and glass, have you seen it? A world of windows and Charles is taking me today.

LOVELACE. Please stop this, Ada.

ADA. He's going to miss me if I'm not there. And the children. No one should miss their father.

ANABELLA. Their father?

LOVELACE. It's the laudanum. She's delirious, she doesn't know what she's saying.

ANABELLA. What do you mean their father?

LOVELACE. I do not want to hear her ramblings, I just want her to sleep.

ANABELLA. The soul cannot rest unconfessed.

LOVELACE. She's not confessing, she's drunk. *(Turning to Ada... prompting her.)*

ADA. Do you know Charles? A great man. He builds engines and I tell them what to do. Do you know our Engine can sing? Birds and machines.

LOVELACE. Ada, please—

ANABELLA. And you confess your love for that man then?

LOVELACE. *I will not have you fuel this fantasy in her.*

ADA. When we met we danced with no music. But I imagined the music. I hear it still. Do you hear it? It's in the in-between of things. That's where love is. And every other impossible thing. You know you've made it there when you can hear the song. *(To Lovelace, like he's someone new and unknown. He is instantly devastated.)* Can you hear it, sir?

> *Lovelace puts all his life into one look at her face.*
> *Then turns on her.*

ANABELLA. God will purify her now.

LOVELACE. I don't care what he does with her. You're the lady of this house now.

CHARLES. *(Offstage—banging on the front door.)* Lord Lovelace. Lady Byron, please—

ANABELLA. God help us. It's him again.

LOVELACE. You know she asked me to be buried next to her father in Hucknall. Her father. Not near you, nor I, nor her children but the man she only knew in…myth. She'd rather that than the life we gave her. That says something about her doesn't it. Or us.

> *More knocking from outside.*

Let him in.

ANABELLA. I will not.

LOVELACE. Just let him in.

ANABELLA. Not when she's just cleansed her soul of him.

LOVELACE. She needed and hated you in equal parts. You know this, don't you?

ANABELLA. *Excuse me.*

ADA. Are you a nice man, sir?

LOVELACE. What?

ADA. I think I know you and I think I know that you are good.

LOVELACE. Very few people are in the end.

ADA. Oh. Is this the end? I have a book I'd like to take with me.

> *Ada reveals the pieced-back-together book of her father's poems from the very first scene. She's kept it all these years.*
>
> *Anabella doesn't know what to say.*
>
> *Charles knocks on the interior door—he's right outside.*

LOVELACE. *(To Charles.)* COME IN. *(To Anabella.)* Someone should be here who cares.

> *Charles enters as Lovelace exits.*

CHARLES. Sir, if I may please say that—

LOVELACE. You may not.

> *Lovelace goes for good. Exits with a slam.*

ANABELLA. Mr. Babbage, for god's sake.

CHARLES. Lady Byron. I will see this woman and there is no respectable reason why you should stop me.

ADA. Darling, I was going to meet you at the Crystal Palace.

ANABELLA. You should have stopped yourself, Mr. Babbage. From the beginning you should have been a gentleman and a—

CHARLES. I was never any other kind of man to her.

ADA. The whole place is glass. The whole thing's a prism.

ANABELLA. You should have let her go.

ADA. Rainbows and light.

ANABELLA. She was never going to leave you, the grand man of science, the father she never had. You should have done the honorable thing and left. her. alone. Now look at her. Abandoned and ruined. Laudanum's on the table. I'll be outside.

ADA. Goodbye madam.

> *Anabella leaves.*

(To Charles.) I don't much care for her really.

CHARLES. Ada, my dear. What can I do? I came every day, she wouldn't let me in.

ADA. We were going to the Crystal Palace today. Because the whole thing's a prism. And our boys will see the future.

CHARLES. What's this now?

ADA. But I can't play the piano anymore. My fingers are stuck. And the music is coming. Can you hear it?

CHARLES. Music?

ADA. Yes. You see there is music in everything. Because there is mathematics in everything. Hidden all around us like a prism hides a rainbow. Until it lets the colors free. I wrote a poem about a rainbow. It's rather good I think. My father's a poet. I'm meeting him at the Crystal Palace.

> *She gets up trying to find the paper—the pain, even on drugs, overwhelms her.*
> *She clutches him. Breathes through it, whimpers.*
> *He holds her.*

CHARLES. I'm here. I'm right here. Why don't we rest—

> *He helps her lie back down.*

ADA. Before we go to the Crystal Palace.

> *Will he play this fantasy with her? Yes.*

CHARLES. Yes. Before we go we'll rest.

ADA. And...what will we do there?

CHARLES. We will...walk.

ADA. Under the glass?

CHARLES. Yes. And by the fountain.

ADA. I do so love the fountain.

CHARLES. So we'll sit by the fountain.

ADA. And wait for the boys. They'll want their father to show them all the feats of wonder.

CHARLES. Yes. The boys will meet us there. And our girls, of course. Three boys and six girls.

ADA. That many?

CHARLES. Oh yes. Our house was overflowing.

ADA. Was it? It was. Yes it was.

CHARLES. It was.

61

ADA. The children. You must find them and show them what we've made. The engine and the music and the children must be shown the future.

CHARLES. The future.

ADA. Yes. It will be lovely I think.

She is fading—tired—

I think I'll rest. And then we'll go. To the future.

CHARLES. Perhaps I'll sit here with you. If that's all right?

ADA. Of course my darling, that'd be lovely.

She kisses his cheek like a wife would.

CHARLES. Would you like a poem? A poem might be just the thing to help you rest.

ADA. Did you know that poems have heartbeats? My father taught me that. There's a bit of maths to them too. One*Two*, One*Two*.

Babbage picks up her father's book. From now on Charles cannot hear Ada.

Like the beginning of the play she taps her chest like a heartbeat along with the iambic cadence of the poem that Charles now reads to her.

Over the next pages Ada gradually turns back into herself... though Charles doesn't notice.

CHARLES.
She walks in beauty, like the night
Of cloudless climes and starry skies;

And all that's best of dark and bright

Meet in her aspect and her eyes:
Thus mellow'd to that tender light
Which heaven to gaudy day denies.

ADA. *(A numeric heartbeat.)*
One*Two*, One*Two*, One*Two*, One*Two*...

One*Two*, One*Two*, One*Two*, One—

Ada is not delirious now, she is fully herself again. She has a thought, Charles cannot not hear or see her.

ADA. Oh dear god. What if...what if...

CHARLES. One shade the more, one ray the less,

ADA. What if the number *system* is what's stopping us.

CHARLES. Had half impaired the nameless grace

ADA. What if we changed the decimals to—

CHARLES. Which waves in every raven tress,

ADA. Yes. We could increase the memory if there's only—oh that could work.

CHARLES. Or softly lightens o'er her face;

ADA. With only *two* symbols it could recycle more commands, more results, it could process faster—

CHARLES. Where thoughts serenely sweet express

ADA. Two numbers, not ten.

CHARLES. How pure, how dear their dwelling-place.

ADA. On, off; hole, covered; one, two—

CHARLES.
And on that cheek, and o'er that brow,
So soft, so calm, yet eloquent,
The smiles that win, the tints that glow,
But tell of days in goodness spent,

ADA.
No. Of course it's not.
Obviously.
It's not one and *two*…

ADA. It's one and *zero*…

CHARLES. A mind at peace with all below,

ADA. Zero and one…

CHARLES. A heart whose love is—

ADA. *(Standing with more energy, more herself every minute.)* Over and over in every combination, for every command in the world. That's it, that's the…

> *But Charles doesn't see her standing. He sees her still lying down…not moving…*
> *She also sees that she has stopped the heartbeat she was tapping on her chest.*
> *She knows what this means.*

The future.

> *Charles stands sharply—looks "at Ada" lying on the couch, even though she stands next to him. To Charles Ada is gone. He catches his breath. Gone. Then he sits next to her. Can't move.*

Ada realizes she's gone too.

She can only look at her soul mate from afar now, even though she's so close.

Now what the hell does she do.

As the world around them changes, fades away. It suffuses with...
Light. Prism-inflected rainbows flicker about her. This place is in between the others...

The Crystal Palace...

Charles takes no note of it...never leaving "Ada's" side. He is in the world she just left...

Is this...the future?

Into this in-between walks...a man.

BYRON. I'm not exactly sure. Feels more like nostalgia to me. Or poetry?

ADA. Excuse me.

BYRON. They're very similar. Lots of pining, nothing to be done. Rather lovely though.

ADA. Did you say Poetry?

BYRON. Yes I can't seem to escape it.
No matter what I do, everything ends up verse. Hello.

ADA. Hello. You're a poet?

BYRON. Precisely. Or regrettably if you're my wife.

ADA. I'm sorry. I...

BYRON. What?

ADA. Oh dear. Are you...Mr. Byron?

BYRON. No. I am *Lord* Byron, a title I, in the traditional English manner, did very little to deserve. And you are?

She is stunned.

Forgive me, do I offend you? Have we met? Or fought? Or...?

ADA. No. I...no, we haven't met. Exactly. Once, I'm told, but not... I'm so sorry I'm at a loss for our...exact...function.

BYRON. I'm sorry, a function?

ADA. A relationship involving one or more variables. It's a metaphor.

BYRON. I'm usually quite good with those but you put me at a loss, my dear.

She thinks...then recites...

ADA.
    "Is thy face like thy mother's, my fair child!   BYRON.
    ADA! sole daughter of my house and heart?   Ada.
    When last I saw thy young blue eyes they smiled,   Ada.
    And then we parted,—"

BYRON. Dear god, child. Ada?

ADA. Correct.

BYRON. Oh my dear.

ADA. Also correct. I suppose. Hello.

BYRON. Hello.

    Pause.

I have...thought of you. Often. Very often.

ADA. Likewise. Well. Three nights in five. Or four in seven. The percentage is certainly in your favor but I'm afraid it's not one hundred.

BYRON. So she turned you into a mathematician? To spite me? She did, didn't she?

ADA. I'm afraid so. Even geography was too potent a subject.

BYRON. What did geography ever do to her?

ADA. Gave you more places to run to. She turned me into a scientist.

BYRON. And what in god's name is that?

ADA. An explorer of the fundamental principles of the universe. Like I'm told a poet is of the heart.

    That pleases him to hear.

BYRON. You speak very well. I'll take credit for that. Did you read my poem?

ADA. Yes. I've read them all.

BYRON. I wrote about you.

ADA. I realized that. Once Mother told me who you were.

BYRON. Which took how long?

ADA. Eighteen years.

BYRON. That woman.

ADA. She was not a fan.

BYRON. I married the one person I couldn't charm.

ADA. Why did you do that?

BYRON. Why *did* I do that?

ADA. She's not very nice.

BYRON. Well, neither was I. We all have our magnetisms and our mistakes.

ADA. Sometimes that seems to be all we have.

BYRON. It certainly tends to be all we remember.

ADA. Memory taunts me. What could have been but wasn't.

BYRON. That's not memory then. That's regret.

ADA. I have never found them separate.

BYRON. You have a shadow to you, my dear.

ADA. *(Starting to turn on him, mad, resentful—)* Yes, well, perhaps you should take credit for that too.

BYRON. Excuse me?

ADA. Actually you'll need to excuse me. I am about to repeat what I know about you and to most people it will seem like a torrent of insult, but I wish to hear from you what is true.

BYRON. You needn't say any more.

ADA. You know of which you're accused? Adultery and abandonment—leaving your women and daughters across Europe to fend for themselves while you prance off to the next bed.

BYRON. I have never pranced in my life.

66

ADA. And that's not even the worst of it. Not the even the worst—

BYRON. I know what you're going to say, you don't have to—

ADA. Is it true?

BYRON. Oh for god's sake—

ADA. *Incest.*

BYRON. *She was a HALF sister—No one was hurt.*

ADA. *(Fighting him, blaming him, calling him out.)* I was hurt—I was. Everyone thinking my father disgusting and disgraceful and that all of that was in me waiting to bleed out. I spent my life glared at or gawked at or gossiped about. I couldn't live my life because of yours.

BYRON. *And why was that?*

ADA. *Because I was your daughter and not your son.*

Byron hears and understands her. He takes a new approach.

BYRON. The human condition is spent along the tight wire between want and ought, what we crave and what's expected. I would not live a life of expectation certainly if it was not my own making. *Nor should you.* To live for passion, to live at *all*, that was a choice I made and I could not have made any other. Your mother knew that my wandering was inevitable. She knew it and she waited for it and she lived drunk off of her dramatic suffering in spite of it.

But I was always wandering back to you. I just never quite made it.

ADA. Why not.

BYRON. Because I've always been the most comfortable…amiss.

ADA. "Amiss" is your excuse? For blackening my life, for leaving me never knowing if I was—

BYRON. I'm sorry.

ADA. I never knew—

BYRON. I'm sorry.

ADA. *I never knew if I was real to you.* Do you know what that's like? Not knowing if you're real or a dash of fiction in your father's mind? *It's unhealthy.*

BYRON. *Might it also have made you unusually comfortable with the power of imagination to set the world on fire.*

67

Pause.

ADA. *(Pissed.)* I'm not sure if you are defying my expectations or perfectly adhering to them.

BYRON. I will excavate a compliment in that.
And attempt to convey my...apologies. Oh god I don't know—What is the etiquette of this? For leaving you, my dear, I am sorry. But I think we both must acknowledge that I would have likely made your life much darker in the end. I tend to do that.

ADA. I just...wanted some of your...greatness. In my life, in *me*. And I might be the only woman in England that doesn't care what you did. You were a great mind, a great man.

BYRON. Yes. Just not a good one.

> *Pause.*
> *She breaks—weeps—she lets it all out—her pain, her regret—he goes to her instinctively. Holds her like a...father.*
> *She accepts this embrace immediately—she needs it so much—but he is shocked by it—by his paternalism, his caring.*

ADA. I've been in such true pain for so long...and I suddenly realized I wasn't.

> *This is very important to him suddenly. He focuses just on her.*

BYRON. I never imagine you hardened, or sad, or lonely. In my mind you're still a child with no worry.

ADA. You missed the middle bit then.

BYRON. I meant that I tried to imagine you happy, I wished for that for you.

ADA. Wishes are rather useless things I find. There is no metal to them.

BYRON. *(Luddite in full.)* A metal wish? Doesn't that sound like a nightmare.

ADA. Does it?

BYRON. *Yes.* Yes it does. Dear god I hope you're not one of those modernists.

ADA. Of course I am. Who's *not* a modernist that doesn't hope to see the future? Machines *are* that future.

BYRON. Like hell they are. You cannot make things better than people.

ADA. But people can make things to better the world.

BYRON. Machines cannot better us, if they've got no heart. Machines cannot love.

ADA. Good for them.

BYRON. You would really want that? To be heartless and cold?

ADA. Painless and unburdened, yes I rather think I would've preferred that.

BYRON. And this from the daughter of a Romantic.

ADA. From a daughter who trusted numbers more than people. Numbers do not lie, nor leave, nor die.

> *Impressed pause. Byron looks at her, really looks.*
> *Drops the charming poet bit…honest and true.*

BYRON. I like you very much. Most people can't say that of their children.

> *An honest flood. He is not charming her with this, he is confessing.*

Had I known you. The words I would have spilt. For you. A million verses vanished when I left your side, and I see it now, and it is agony to imagine them.

> *This means so much to her. But she can't help the tease.*

ADA. I will excavate a compliment in that.

BYRON. There is truly no higher one that I have. Truly.

> *Ada is so struck by this she confesses as well…*

ADA. You know I…I don't exactly know why but I…asked to end up next to you.
In case you wonder whom that strange girl is beside you. It's me.

> *He hugs her again. Really starting to feel the pride and pull of a parent.*

BYRON. I know it's you. I know you and you are not alone, my beautiful, brilliant, impossible girl. And you are free. And you are free. And now you are free.

> *He starts to release her—but she holds him fast, not letting him go, needing him more. This is what he can do for her. She has a thought…*

ADA. Here I always thought true freedom was impossible.

BYRON. Not everything that seems impossible stays impossible.

The idea lands on her, strikes her, she is held in awe.

ADA. Oh my god.

What if he built it? He actually built it.

BYRON. Built what?

ADA. Or someone did.

BYRON. Built *what*?

ADA. *(So proud of Charles.)* The Engine. It could…if he made it, it could…hold the past, present, and future. Together. Like it seems to be doing right now.

BYRON. I'm sorry, did you say an *engine*? Like a train or—?

ADA. Like a mind.

BYRON. *(Deeply skeptical.)* An engine with a mind?

ADA. No. The Engine *is* the mind.

BYRON. Which is all the more impossible.

ADA. *(Agreeing.)* Isn't it?

Talking about them, together, talking right now.

Isn't *this*? Impossible things don't stay impossible. Once you can imagine it then they start to exist. What if *it* exists—now it exists, which is why *we* exist, which is why we're here at all!

BYRON. Which would make all a figment of someone's imagination?

ADA. Yes. And computation.

Ada looks around the room.

She must experiment to know for sure.

So she does…offering the space a tentative…

One.

The space chimes one note. Confirmation. My god she's right.
As soon as it confirms her thesis she is thinking at light speed,
from this point until the song starts the lines are fast, urgent,
pick up cues, go go go—

(To him.) Do you hear that? *Can you hear it?*

BYRON. Yes, but—

ADA. *(To the machine.)* Zero!

    The note silences. Another confirmation for Ada!

BYRON. What is that, what are you doing?

ADA. *(To him.)* I don't know but— *(To the machine.)* One!

    Another note! Yes!

(Back to him—) I think I might be programming it to make music.

BYRON. Programming what?

    ADA. The Engine!

        BYRON. The Engine makes—?

            ADA. Yes! Music!

(To the machine.) Zero!

    The note silences. She is loving this!

BYRON. But where is it coming from?

ADA. *(To the machine.)* One!

    Another note!

The same place *we're* coming from— *(To the machine.)* Zero!

    No note.

(Back to him.) the in-between of things, the impossible future that isn't impossible!

BYRON. And you're programming the impossible?

ADA. Well. Someone has to teach it to sing. *(To the machine.)* One.

    Then...

    The Engine suddenly starts up around them—music and machinery.

    They are inside the memory of the Analytical Engine. They are part of the machine, which clanks and clamors with metal on metal sounds wrapping them in.

    They marvel at this.

    They exist together in this space, this sound, this impossibility.

    Their song starts. His is poetry, hers is binary...

    They dance as they sing and the Analytical Engine whirs and clanks around them.

ADA. *(Sung—rubato.)* and all the gears are spinning round
they spiral up, they tumble down
it fills the room this dream of mine
the numbers falling into line

    Piano arpeggio 1x alone.

ADA. she walks
in beauty
like
the night

of cloudless
climes
and
starry

ski—i—i—i—ies…

and all the gears
are spinning round

              BYRON. she walks
              in beauty
they spiral up,   like
they tumble dow—   the night
    ow—own…

              of cloudless
              climes
              and
              starry
it fills the room
this dream of mine   ski—i—i—i—ies…

              she walks
              in beauty
              like   *Babbage sings of*
the numbers   the night   *their machine.*
falling into li—i—   *He can see Ada*

i—ine...

one zero, zero, one.

one, one
one zero, zero, one.

one, one
one zero, zero, one.

one, one
one zero, zero, one.

one, one
one zero, zero, one.

one, one
one zero, zero, one.

of cloudless
climes
and
starry
ski—i—i—i—ies...

she walks
in beauty
like
the night

of cloudless
climes
and
starry

ski—i—i—i—ies...

she walks
in beauty
like
the night

of cloudless
climes
and
starry

ski—i—i—i—ies...

again in this
dream...

CHARLES.
and all the gears
are spinning round
they spiral up,
they tumble down

it fills the room
this dream of mine
the numbers
falling into line

and all the gears
are spinning round
they spiral up,
they tumble down

it fills the room
this dream of mine
the numbers
falling into line

and all the gears
are spinning round
they spiral up,
they tumble down

it fills the room
this dream of mine
the numbers
falling into line

and all the gears
are spinning round
they spiral up,
they tumble down

it fills the room
this dream of mine
the numbers
falling into line

Byron touches Ada goodbye for now.
As she turns her attention to Babbage:

one,
one,
zero.

one,
one,
zero

one,
one,
zero

one,
one,
zero—

one,
one,
zero,
one,
one,
one,
zero
one,
one,
one—

she walks
in beauty
like
the night

of cloudless
climes
and
starry
skies…

Babbage says goodbye too—doesn't want to, must leave her.

ADA. all the stars
and all the clocks
and all the lines
and where they cross

and all the clouds
and all the trees

and all the spaces
in between

and all the birds
and all the bells
and all the stories
they can tell

and all the steam
and all the steel
and all the secrets
they conceal

all the stars
and all the clocks
and all the lines
and where they cross

and all the clouds
and all the trees
and all the spaces
in between

and all the birds
and all the bells
and all the stories
they can tell

and all the steam
and all the steel
and all the secrets
they reveal

and now the world
is fading white
numbers spinning
into light

and now the world
is fading white
numbers spinning into…

> Ada is alone…her ones and zeros now echoing around her, outside of her. She is not singing but sound is all around her.

> The song and the numbers funnel down into a spotlight on her.

> The spotlight and song gradually fade as a strange blue light and a strange new sound takes over…

> It's the blue light of modern computer screens—laptops, iPhones, iPads—all giving off their ghostly light on her.

> All playing her song.

> Blackout.

End of Play

PROPERTY LIST
(Use this space to create props lists for your production)

SOUND EFFECTS
(Use this space to create sound effects lists for your production)

Note on Songs/Recordings, Images, or Other Production Design Elements

The rights to perform "Ada's Vision" by The Kilbanes are included with written performance licenses for this play. Licensees of the Play are required to give the following credit in all programs, and wherever other designers receive credit, in size and prominence of type equal to that used for the designers:

Original music composed by The Kilbanes

Be advised that Dramatists Play Service, Inc., neither holds the rights to nor grants permission to use any songs, recordings, images, or other design elements mentioned in the play, other than the aforementioned "Ada's Vision." It is the responsibility of the producing theater/organization to obtain permission of the copyright owner(s) for any such use. Additional royalty fees may apply for the right to use copyrighted materials.

For any songs/recordings, images, or other design elements mentioned in the play except for "Ada's Vision," works in the public domain may be substituted. It is the producing theater/organization's responsibility to ensure the substituted work is indeed in the public domain. Dramatists Play Service, Inc., cannot advise as to whether or not a song/arrangement/recording, image, or other design element is in the public domain.